iOS

Programming

For Beginners:

The Ultimate iOS App Developer's Guide

By

Joseph Joyner

Table of Contents

iOS Programming For Beginners: The Ultimate iOS App Developer's Guide

By Joseph Joyner

First Published, 2015

Printed in the United States of America

Part 1. iOS Basics

iOS that is previously known as iPhone OS is a popular mobile operating system developed and distributed exclusively by Apple Inc for Apple hardware. Recently, this operating system has gained much popularity in the mobile world because of its high modern technology. It's the only operating system in the market that provides power to many company's iDevices.

Though it has unveiled for the iPhone in 2007, it has broadened its outlook in a very quick moment and started to support other Apple based devices like the iPod Touch in September 2007, iPad in January 2010 and iPad mini in November 2012.

Activities:

The iOS user interface is fully based on the idea of direct manipulation and exploration, using multi-touch signals. Interface managing elements include switches, sliders, and buttons. Interface with the operating system contains gestures such as pinch, swipe, tape and also reverse pinch, all of which have exact introductions within the milieu of the iOS and its multi-touch boundary or interface. Core accelerometers are often used and utilized by several applications to react to trembling the device or rotating it in 3 dimensions.

Frameworks for iOS Development:

IOS shares with OS X various frameworks, for example Foundation and Core Foundation. Still, its user interface toolkit is Cocoa Touch. As a result, it gives or offers the UIKit framework than the AppKit framework or structure. It is then not well-suited with OS X for many applications. Also, while iOS operating system share the Darwin foundation with Operating System X, Unix-like shell entrée is not presented to users and limited to applications, making iOS not complete Unix-compatible either. The iPhone OS Core Services Layer and The iPhone OS Media Layer are included in the framework as well.

Architecture of iOS:

The iPhone has a very similar architecture with Android (The most popular operating system currently). The iPhone operating system includes a number of software layers, each of which offers programming frameworks in an outstanding way for the development of mobile applications that simply run on top of the OS.

Some figures designed to graphically represent the software stack of the OS explain an additional box placed above the Cocoa Touch layer to designate the applications successively running on the machine. In practice, an app can easily and directly call any of the software layers of the stack to carry out tasks on the device.

That supposed, still, each operating system layer offers a rising level of concept away from the difficulty of working with the hardware or physical part. You should, then, constantly look for answers to your programming purposes in the frameworks placed in the advanced level operating system layers before starting code to write that accomplishes to the lower level layers. Generally, the highest level of software layer you program too, the less attempt and least number of lines of code you will have to inscribe to attain your goal. And as any expert programmer will advise you, the less code you need to write, the less chance you have to set up bugs.

Multitasking:

Multitasking is a significant topic in iOS. Multitasking is the process of performing a number of tasks concurrently. It was first released in iOS in June 2010 together with iOS 4.0. Only definite devices—iPhone 3GS, iPhone 4, and iPod Touch 3rd generation—were capable of using multitasking. The iPad did not acquire multitasking until the discharge of iOS 4.2.1 in 2010. At this time, multitasking is fully supported, compatible and used on the iPhone 3GS or newer versions, iPod Touch 3rd generation or newer versions, and the entire iPad models.

Completion of multitasking in the IOS operating system has been disapproved for its approach, that restricts the work that apps in the background can carry out a limited function set, and for having need of application developers to adjoin clear support for it.

Before the release of iOS 4, multitasking was very restricted to a collection of the apps Apple integrated in the device. Users could, yet "jailbreak" their mobile device in order to informally multitask. After releasing the most comprehensive iOS 4, on 3rd generation and newer devices, multitasking is actually supported through these 7 background Application Programming Interfaces.

1. Background audio – Here application runs in the background of the device provided that it is playing video or audio content

2. Background location – This notifies the change of location.

3. Voice over IP –When a phone call is not started, the application is suspended.

4. Push notifications

5. Fast application switching – app does not carry out any code and may be eliminated from remembrance at any time

6. Local notifications –local notifications to be transported at a fixed time

7. Task completion – In the device, the application requests the system for additional time to finish a specified task

New background APIs in iOS 5:

1. Newsstand – Through this API, an application can easily download the necessary data in the background to be prepared for the user

2. Bluetooth Accessory – With the help of this API, application confers with a Bluetooth accessory and also can share data at usual intervals

3. External Accessory – Here, app confers with an outer accessory. Then it shares and confers data at regular intervals without facing any problem with the connection.

To make iOS more advanced than before, Apple introduced a fresh multitasking feature in iOS 7, giving all applications with the capability to execute background updates. This trait prefers to modernize the user's most regularly used apps and likes to use WiFi networks over a mobile cellular network, without noticeably decreasing the device's battery life and maintains longer life.

Part 2. Developing an Application in iOS

Installation Requirements in iOS Platform:

Before starting your life as an iOS developer or making a MAF application, make sure that every piece of the software is available in your computer:

a) A desktop or laptop running Apple Mac Operating System X and version will be 10.9.5 or later version

b) Oracle JDeveloper

c) Xcode and iOS SDK

d) Oracle JDeveloper addition for MAF

Here, the last topic we describe is the most needed tools to develop MAF application because now, most of the developers use it for developing.

Before you start:

1. Download the latest version of JDK 1.7 and install it on your computer.

JDeveloper requires this version of JDK

2. Download the latest version of JDK 1.8 and then install it.

The MAF extension needs this version of JDK

3. Download the latest JDeveloper 12.1.3.0.0 (Studio Edition).

In the windows platform, to install JDeveloper use the following:

a) In the file system, find the way to the directory that holds the JDeveloper executable file, after that right-click on the folder and select CMD Prompt window.

b) Then run the command to clearly install JDeveloper using the necessary JDK 1.7:

Enter the JDK7 path separated by '_' then use a backslash ("\"), then bin and again backslash. Writer Java-jar and again backslash and lastly use <JDEV_12.1.3_jar>

In the MAC platform, to install JDeveloper use the following criteria:

1) Firstly, open a window.

2) Put the JAVA_HOME to Java 1.7 and run the command described in the following:

Write export JAVA_HOME then uses a "=" sign. After that, use a "$" sign and first left parenthesis and then type '/usr/libexec/java_home -v1.7' and close the right parenthesis.

3) Make sure that Java 1.7 is running by using the command given in the following:

Java -version

4) Install JDeveloper uses the same window by executing the following line in the command prompt:

Java -jar <JDEV_12.1.3_jar>

To verify where the JDeveloper is installed correctly or not, use the following:

1. Ensure the <JDEV_HOME>\jdev\bin\ jdev.conf file. You can find it in JDEV_HOME then jdev, further bin and next the desired file and verify that the SetJavaHome attributes indicates JDK 1.7.

2. Initiate JDeveloper and choose the Studio Developer role when provoked.

3. In the menu bar, choose Help and then about and finally version and make sure that the java platform 1.7 is applied and used.

Install the MAF Extension:

You can download the MAF extension. You get this option by clicking the check for updates menu.

Once you have set up the extension, you have to configure other development instruments for the following platforms where you tend to install your MAF application.

For the downloading process and installation procedure, use the steps:

1. In JDeveloper, select Help and then Check for Updates.

Special notes:

You might require to configure some proxy settings on your computer: to do it on Windows, choose Tools >

Preferences, and then Web Browser and Proxy that is found in the left of the Preferences dialog; to do it on Mac OS X as well, you will get this on JDeveloper > Preferences. Now; you have set proxy successfully.

2. In the Select update source page, you will see some basic update options. Select Official Oracle Extensions in the select update source page and Updates and click Next.

On the other hand, if network access is absent, you can choose the Install. You will get it in Local File option. Now, you need to indicate to the MAF extension file what you have already downloaded. Show the path of the directory.

Select and choose the Mobile Application Framework update from the selective updates install dialogue.

3. After completing all of them, click I Agree button.

4. Then click Next, and last of all click Finish.

5. Start again JDeveloper by closing all of the tabs.

6. Click on the Create JDK 8 Profile dialog and give the appropriate path to the directory on your laptop or desktop computer that holds JDK 1.8.

Another note:

If you give an unacceptable or unwanted directory that does not have JDK 1.8, an error dialog will be displayed.

Here, you do not need to complete or finish the Create JDK 8 Profile dialog again, you use JDeveloper, unless you re-setup the MAF extension and select not to conserve JDeveloper's system preferences.

1. Verify whether or not the MAF extension has been fruitfully included to JDeveloper:

A. Choose File > New > then From Gallery to open or execute the New Gallery dialog.

B. Expand the Client Tier node from the left on the categories and ensure that It has Mobile Application Framework

Besides, ensure again that you set up the right version of MAF extensions. To do so, choose Help and then

About from the main menu, next choose the Extensions tab, and then inspect the extension list accesses by probing for Mobile Application Framework.

Installing SDK:

1. Once the downloading process is complete or finished, try to search for where the .dmg file was downloaded. Double-click on it and open the image of the disk.

2. Click on the installer package, then which will be found inside of the image. The installer will start and let you to set up the SDK. You don't need to do much then, just follow the instructions on the screen. Always remember that setting up the SDK will take space about 2-3GBs of your hard disk; you can set up the SDK on an outer hard drive if needed.

Once the setup is completed, you will see that a "Developer" folder will be on the top point of your hard drive. You will get the main tools or instruments that are used to make iPhone apps in this folder.

Integrated Development Environment:

Apple's IDE or Integrated Development Tool for both iOS apps and Mac is Xcode. It's totally free and easy to write code and check. You can easily download it from Apple's official site. Xcode is the IDE and is one of the best graphical interfaces for the coders to write code. It's also an exceptional tool for beginners who can understand the function quite easily. You will get everything here to write for iOS 8 with new software languages of Apple. It's only available and present for Mac as well, so if you develop an idea of creating iOS apps, you'll require to be running OS X.

As Apple develops many software languages, you can program iOS in many languages (accepted language from Apple) including Objective C (A quite popular language)

API Capabilities:

Apple, one of the leading corporations has a ton of APIs to entrée app extensions, Photos, Touch ID, HealthKit, and more. Make acquainted yourself with these so you can incorporate more advanced traits into your application.

WatchKit:

Beginning early 2015, you will be capable of delivering innovative experiences on Apple. See that re-imagine and improve the functionality and technology of your iPhone applications. WatchKit offers three beautiful opportunities to expand your iPhone application to Apple Watch: WatchKit applications, actionable notifications, and Glances.

Touch ID:

Your application can use Touch ID to validate a user before using some or all documents in your app. Moreover, fingerprint data is fully protected and never used by iOS or other applications. And with the function of Apple Pay, users can hurriedly and securely pay for physical services with only a single touch on the screen.

PhotoKit:

PhotoKit offers new APIs for efficiently working with video assets and photo, that are controlled by the

Photos app. So, it's possible to can edit photos in the Camera roll directly from your app without having to bring in them first. Key characteristics contain a thread-safe architecture for getting and caching thumbnails or full-sized photos, giving requests for changes to assets, seeing changes that are made by other applications, and resemble editing of asset data.

HealthKit:

HealthKit permits applications, offering health and fitness services to use shared health-related tidings. A user's health news is captured and stored in a centralized and protected location and the user takes the decision on which data should be doled with your application.

Your application has the power to access any health-related news and can give information and news about the user without you require implementing support for fitness-tracking devices. News can come from devices easily that is connected to an iOS or manual access by the user.

HomeKit:

HomeKit is an updated and new version of the framework that is needed for communicating with and managing connected devices in a home (user's home). Your application can enable users to find out devices in their home and organize them, or you can generate actions to manage those devices quite effectively. Users can combine actions together and activate them using Siri.

Defining Swift- A New Programming Language:

Swift is the Apple's recent programming language. It is made especially for Macs and iOS. It's allegedly much simpler to work with and of course use, so if you're completely new to this iOS development, it's really a very good idea to start with this language. It generally works with and is extremely similar to Objective-C

Swift is an inventive new language for programming area and for Cocoa and Cocoa Touch. Actually writing code is very interesting and fun. Only coders who are familiar with coding and expert in coding know how much interest they get when their code. The syntax is shorter yet expressive, and applications run lightning-fast. Now, Swift is completely ready to start and also for your iOS and OS X project.

Swift has many other traits to make your code easier-to-read:

A. Generics

B. Closures combined with function pointers

C. Multiple and Tuples return values

D. Structs that hold methods, protocols, extensions.

F. Fast and brief iteration over a range

F. Functional programming patterns

Install Xcode:

The first and foremost thing you need to perform is set up a free program that is known as Xcode. It is an Integrated Development Environment of Apple, or short form is IDE, which is the major tool you'll have to use to make your iOS apps. Now you have done almost everything to start a new app. Your first project will be a Mac OS X command-line application. You can create or make this project using Objective c, Swift etc.

So, it's time to start now. First of all, start Xcode, and you'll get a window. Then you will get a button that notifies Create a new Xcode project, which is located under the Welcome to Xcode title,

You can create or start a new project if you If you close the window welcome to Xcode by mistake. To start, you have go to the File menu and choosing New > Project....

After that click on Applications and choose Command Line Tool which can be found in your left side

Fill all the fields just like that.

1) Product Name: First Project on iOS

2) Organization Name: It can be left blank. You can also enter the company name if you wish

3) Type: Foundation

4) Company Identifier: Write com.yourname, like com.Stanley

5) Use Automatic Reference Counting: Click to Check this box

Click Next. Select a location to accumulate the project files, and click Create. Then Xcode will install your new project and start it in the editor to do coding for you.

To run code in Xcode, you have to do the following:

1. Open Xcode and create a new project.

2. Next, select a single view application

3. After that, enter the fields like products name, company identifier, organization name as described in the above:

4. Make sure that automatic reference counting is chosen to release the resources automatically allocated once it goes out of range. Then Click Next.

5. Choose the directory for the project and then choose create.

6. Now choose iPhone simulator and select run.

The Structure of Your Source Code:

Now start with the code. Suppose, 'main.m' is the actual source code of your new application. As I have described earlier, how to open a project in Xcode. So, I would like to start with the source code here. It is like a record of instructions to inform the computer what you need it to perform.

Again, a computer cannot directly run source code without instructions or without the help of compilers. Computers only know a language which is known as machine code, so there requires being an intermediate step to change your high-level source code into machine code instructions that the CPU can execute. Xcode performs this when it actually builds and runs your application by compiling source code. This step compiles the source code and makes the corresponding machine code. Machine code is the code of 0 and 1 and we all know that computers don't know anything else than only 0 and 1. So, it's needed to be converted anything to machine code to make computers understand.

You can see a number of lines starting with two slashes (//).

These lines are called comments. These are used to understand the other's code and make it understand and clear to everyone quite easily. It is actually ignored by the compiler. They might find useful when there have been some problems and leave it to experts to solve. Comments are also used in various purposes which can't be described easily. Here we are going to give you a perfect example and we are quite sure that you don't have problems with comments.

```
// insert code in this place...
```

```
NSLog(@"you can write or code anything!");
```

The comment is totally ignored by the compiler when building and running. It was placed there by some obliging engineer at Apple to assist you realize the code and get started from that line.

Import Statements:

```
#import <Foundation/Foundation.h>
```

That code is called an import statement. When coding with Xcode, not the whole thing has to be included in one file; instead, you can make use of code included in separate files and folders. The import statement notifies the compiler that when app's compilation is done, make use of this code from this file.

As you can visualize, developing for iOS and OS X needs a lot of miscellaneous functionality, ranging from handling text, to making many requests over a network, to getting your location on a map or chart. Rather than contain a real "kitchen sink" of functionality into each application you generate, import statements permit you to choose which traits you need for your application to function. This assists to reduce the size of the code, the processing overhead needed, and compilation time.

Main Function:

Now see the line following the import statement:

After providing the import statement, you need to declare the main function. Below is the main function statement that needs to declare.

int main (parameter, const char * argv[])

It declares a function called main function. The entire code in your application that gives some form of logic or processing is summarized into functions. In a word, the main function is actually the function that kicks off the entire application.

Consider a function as a number of lines in a code that usually accepts input and produces results of the corresponding program. For instance, a function could get an account number, take a look at in a database, and go back to the account holder's name.

Here, int main indicates the return value of main gives an integer such as -2 or 10. The int parameter, const char * argv[] are the inputs or arguments, to the main function. You'll return to the spats of a function quite later on.

After the function there is a curly brace that signifies the beginning of the function. You will see the right brace below the main function. Everything contained in between these two braces is part and parcel of the main function.

Variables:

Computers are dreadfully expert at remembering pieces of news such as dates, photos and names. Variables give ways for you to hoard and direct these kinds of objects in the program. There are 4 basic kinds of variables:

a) int: It stores a full number, for example 1, 487. Floating point numbers can't be included here.

b) float: It stores a floating-point number such as 0.5, 3.16, or 1.43

c) char: It stores only a single character, such as "f", "G", or "L".

d) BOOL: It stores a boolean type value such as yes or no. Other programming languages use TRUE and FALSE.

To generate a variable — also recognized as declaring a variable — you just denote its type, give it a simple name and optionally give a default value.

After that add the code of the line to main.m between the NSLog line and the @autoreleasepool line:

```
int num = 400;
```

Don't fail to remember that all-important semicolon! Otherwise, it will give a syntax error.

Conditionals:

Now, code runs in a linear fashion. But there is a question here. How do you deal with the situation where you require performing various actions?

Think about the plan and design of your pastime for an instant. You have three possible situations that require to be checked, and a set of equivalent actions:

1) The guess is right — applaud the player

2) The guess is too high — notify the player to estimate a lower number

3) The estimate is too low — notify the player to estimate a higher number

Here, conditional statements are very important in programming. They are programming structures that let you to make on-the-fly judgments in your code and alter the flow of the logic of the code. Conditionals perform by determining if a picky set of conditions is false or true. If true, then the app will perform a specific work otherwise not.

Now add the lines below after scanf line:

```
if (guess > the_real_answer) {

  NSLog(@"Lower!"); //print Lower

}

else if (guess < the_real_answer) {

  NSLog(@"Higher!"); // print Higher

}

else {

  NSLog(@"the result is correct! The answer was %i",
the_real_answer);

}
```

Here you see some statements and some logics. If, else, else if are known as a conditional statement. They will have two braces. One is the starting brace and another is the closing braces. The whole condition will lie in between these two braces. Otherwise this will not work properly. You can also change the condition reversely by changing the signs. Again, we have used the scanf function in the above. scanf is used for the input. When guessing something, you need to provide an input as a guess. To give input you have to use this function.

There are also some different comparison operators. You can use them in if statement:

1. > : greater than

2. == : equal to

3. < : less than

4. <= : less than or equal to

5. >= : greater than or equal to

6. != : not equal to

Final Words

But to be a good programmer or a developer in iOS, you need to know the entire things of iOS. Otherwise, you won't get the right path when programming a complex application. Here, this book provides the most basic and fundamental topics of iOS for beginners. Without the knowledge of the above, you can't go a long way where you can produce some extraordinary apps with outstanding thoughts and values.

Thank You Page

I want to personally thank you for reading my book. I hope you found information in this book useful and I would be very grateful if you could leave your honest review about this book. I certainly want to thank you in advance for doing this.

If you have the time, you can check my other books too.

www.ingramcontent.com/pod-product-compliance
Lightning Source LLC
Chambersburg PA
CBHW070906070326
40690CB00009B/2014